Whoa Dog, Whoa!

The Leash Can Be Your Friend

Mike Deathe CPDT-KA

Published by FastPencil Publishing

Whoa Dog, Whoa!

First Edition

Print edition ISBN: 9781499905045

Copyright © KISS Pet Solutions LLC 2018

All rights reserved. No part of this publication may be reproduced, stored in a retrieval system, or transmitted, in any form, or by any means, electronic, mechanical, photocopying, recording, or otherwise, without the prior consent of the publisher.

Sale of this book without a front cover may be unauthorized. If the book is coverless, it may have been reported to the publisher as "unsold or destroyed" and neither the author nor the publisher may have received payment for it.

http://www.fastpencil.com

Printed in the United States of America

Table of Contents

Dedication 5
Introduction 7
A note from your author 9
Why does my dog pull on his or her leash? 11
What are we reinforcing? 13
The Gear 15
Hand Feeding (Gotta have attention to fix a problem) 21
Watch Me 25
Turn-Around Game 29
Leash work in the house 31
Backyard Building Blocks 33
Driveway Distractions and Front Yard Fiascos 37
The actual walking work week 41
The Combo Walk: Putting it all together! 43
Weekend Work 45
My Warranty Statement 47
Conclusion 49

Dedication

This book is for everyone who has ever hated walking their dog! Let's face it: If something is not fun, we are not going to practice, and without practice nothing is going to change! So, my goal is simple: An easy set of steps to get you to practice, improve and have some fun while you are walking your dog. If I can get you to relax a bit and just enjoy the process, I think both you and your pooch can learn to walk together, versus walking against each other.

Poor leash walking is one of the main reasons for dogs being returned or relinquished to local shelters. Teaching good leash skills is my way of keeping more dogs in their Forever Homes.

I would also like to thank all my clients over the last decade, you were the ones that allowed me to learn, explain, teach and show these techniques... You are the one's that proved it works!

Thank you, Eliza Cantlay, for all the editing help; this book would not have been possible without you and Petri!

Mikeal Barnheart, for another awesome cover! (And for not making my hair gray in this version).

I hope you enjoy it!

Mike

Introduction

It's beautiful outside, and a perfect day for a walk! You call for your best four legged friend, hook them up on the leash, and open the door. The next thing you know you are sitting on your butt, shoulder throbbing in pain, and you catch a fleeting glimpse of your dog barreling down the street away from you. You wonder why you even try to walk this damn dog! Every time you try, you end up in pain or tears. At best, you end up holding on for dear life, and praying for the torture to end.

Well if you dread walking your dog, you are reading the right book. *Whoa Dog, Whoa!* will teach you:

- How to make leash training easier.
- How to make leash training more fun.
- And yes, actually show you how to teach your dog to not only slow down, but to pay attention while on leash.

So get up, dust yourself off and let's teach your dog how to walk nicely. Flip the page and let's get this party started!

A Note from Your Author

Leash walking and recall (i.e., coming when called) are very similar skills, and many of their techniques overlap. There are specific things that each skill needs to achieve success. In this book you will read about the use of a long line; and while that is definitely a recall technique, I have found that it works wonders for leash pullers, if taught in tandem with leash techniques.

I highly recommend reading my recall book, *How To Make Your Dog Come Without Being A Butt-Head* before tackling this one. Reading the recall book first will make your journey smoother, and in the end a lot more *fun*... And that, my friends, will be the secret to your success (along with practice). With that being said, let's get to why dogs pull!

Why does my dog pull on his or her leash?

Well the simple answer is... Because it *works*!

Our four-legged canine counterparts only do things that produce a result. If Fido is engaging in a behavior, chances are you are doing something that is reinforcing that behavior, intentionally or not. Dog behavior is easier to predict, manage or modify if you are willing to admit that you are doing something to prompt that behavior!

What does all this mean with a dog who pulls on a leash? If dogs only do what works, (and at this point it must be working or you would not have bought this book!), you are probably caught up in the downward spiral of allowing Fido to create bad habits. Think about it: Whatever you do in life repetitively, you end up getting better at, whether for better or worse. For example:

- Sports
- Lying
- Public speaking
- Driving
- Chewing your fingernails
- Saying "Thank you"

Let's face it: From your dog's perspective, the fastest way to get from point A to point B is to simply drag you along for the ride. So why on earth would the dog slow down? From his or her perspective, they are just saving you time! They have four legs, and you, the silly human, only have two. Fido figures he is just helping you out and getting you there twice as fast. Where's the motivation for the dog to do anything differently?

Now if you are lucky and you have a puppy and are reading this book, great! You can simply teach the right behaviors from the get-go, and in no time your dog will perfect an easy-paced loose leash walk. The rest of you readers no doubt already have pooches who have perfected leash pulling. Ironically, the techniques to teach loose leash walking are the same either way, but if you fall into the second category, be warned: It will take longer.

You will simply create an alternate or replacement behavior to the pulling: We are going to make leash pulling less rewarding than walking with a loose, relaxed leash. Because if we make the leash pulling less rewarding, then the behavior will go away; and this is what we dog trainers like to call the "extinguishment of a behavior".

It really is that simple! But please do not confuse the ideas of quick and simple... If you do everything I discuss in the book, and do it in a consistent and frequent manner, you should be able to see substantial improvement in 6-8 weeks of practice... I said *simple*, not fast!

So, let's look at how you are walking your dog *now*, and see where this wonderfully terrible behavior got its start.

What are we reinforcing?

We start one of two ways... Either we say the words, "Wanna go for a walk?" or we simply grab the leash and next thing we know we have a severe case of our doggie going "B.S.C."

Next we fasten the leash, open the front door and our pooch drags us out the door at high speed. And the walk begins: Dragging, tugging, pulling your slow butt to the next stop on the itinerary. You yell, scream, plead and probably use language that would make your mother blush. But did it stop the pulling? Well if it did, I would imagine you would not be reading this book. In all actuality, your dog probably thinks you are *enjoying* this romp through the neighborhood as much as they are!

The fact remains that *pulling still works*. The dog starts at point A and ends at point B, even with all your objecting and scolding. Even pulling back on the dog seems to have minimal success, because once you release tension or quit jerking the dog, they go right back to pulling. You, my friend, are focused on the behavior you *don't* want, rather than what you *do* want, and that is the little secret within this book. But before we get to the specifics, let's look at some of the tools out there on the market. Some of which I am sure you probably have stuck in some drawer in the house!

*Bat Shit Crazy.

The Gear

Gear that I am not a fan of:

- **Retractable Leashes.**

If I could outlaw any item in dog training it would be the retractable leash. Who came up with the idea of putting dogs on leashes that magically gives them more and more freedom, no matter what their behavior is? Due to the spring action on the leash, there is tension on the dog's neck on the way out, and on the way back in. Retractable leashes work off a spring tension system. As the dog pulls the leash out, the spring is creating tension so that when he or she stops, the spring pulls the excess leash back into the handle (think of a tape measure). There is tension on the dog's neck as he or she moves away from you, and there is tension coming back to you. Why is this a big deal? Because *tension = pulling*: Your dog is learning that pulling is a good thing if you are using this kind of leash.

- **Regular Harness vs. Collar.**

Many folks will switch to a harness thinking it will stop the pulling, but all it does is take the pull off the dog's neck and put it on the shoulders[*]... Which is stronger, the neck or the shoulders? Now for those dogs that gag or choke themselves, switching to a harness can prevent neck and trachea damage, and keep their airways from being compromised; but it will have no effect on pulling.

> ***Trainer's Tip: Brachycephalic dogs (those with smushed noses, like pugs) should always be on harnesses instead of collars. They have a hard enough time breathing. But again... This is not going to improve leash pulling!***

- **Choke chains and Prong collars.**

These devices tend to be controversial in the dog training realm, and this book is from my point of view... So, if you love them, use them, but I do not recommend them. I believe that they are a punitive device, and I preach positive reinforcement training.

Before I get into the specifics, let's switch gears and talk about people:

There are two types of folks, "The Yeller" and "The Teacher". One type is reactive and focuses on mistakes, usually dealing out consequences. The other type is proactive, and makes sure to teach skills first and then reward. The real difference is in what they do when dealing with mistakes: Do they teach or do they punish? Most people would choose The Teacher, and that's what this book and its techniques are all about! The first step has to be teaching the dog the skills we want and expect. Secondly we have to reward the right behavior versus punishing bad behavior. If you don't take the time to teach Fido exactly what you want, how can you expect him to know what to do?

The idea of these tools is to *correct* the dog when they decide to pull, which then should *teach* the dog not to pull.

To me, this is putting the cart before the horse: The first step should be *teaching* not to pull, not correcting the dog for pulling. It's like getting scolded at work for something you didn't even know was your responsibility!

Another thing I've seen humans do that doesn't make sense is that they will often "correct" (ie, jerk the leash) when the leash is slack or loose. So, you end up correcting the dog when the leash is loose; this is actually what you wanted in the first place! In many cases the dog just learns to keep the leash tight so the owner can't correct them.

Remember that training should be fun for both owner and dog. Techniques that focus on what *not* to do (or that get a correction) can make training less fun for both parties, and the likelihood of continuing with the training process long enough to see results is low: Folks just give up, and the dog ends up hating training.

Ironically, most folks who go this route with these devices are usually looking for a quick fix; an instant gratification method. The only thing that trains dogs are consistency and frequency of practice.

The gear I can get on board with:

- **Nose Halter, No-Pull Types:**

These tools look a lot like a halter for a horse, and often work the same way. When the dog pulls, the halter pulls the dog's head sideways, creating mild discomfort. The dog does not like this feeling and chooses to stop pulling, which creates slack or looseness in the leash to stop the discomfort. *This is key: Instead of me having to actively correct my dog for doing something I do not like, I allow the dog to figure out how to make the discomfort of the halter go away, thus learning the correct choice for themselves!* The difference is allowing the dog to do the learning, versus me having to initiate a punishment to learn.

Trainer's Tip: These devices put a lot of pressure on a dog's neck. NEVER jerk, pop or use a leash correction with these devices. You can do severe neck damage. Let the dog do the learning!

A negative side of these tools is that they are so effective, that owners forget to condition the dog to wearing them before starting the training; this leads to a dog that rubs their nose on you or the ground, or even paws at the halter all the time. Anyone familiar with horses would never attempt to bit or bridle train a horse in just one day, but folks do this all the time with this type of device on a dog. Instead we should allow the dog to wear the halter for a week or two (associating it with treats and fun!) before ever attaching the leash, so that we can provide positive associations while wearing the device.

- **Front Load, No-Pull Harnesses**

Back to the Brachycephalic dogs... If you have no real nose to speak of, you can't use a nose halter, can you? Well many of these companies designed harnesses based on the same principles for these dogs! The main difference is a standard harness that hooks up on the dog's back, takes the pull off the neck and puts it on the shoulders. These no-pull harnesses attach at the chest so that each time the dog pulls, their body is turned sideways, so that they lose their forward momentum creating some discomfort. Again, the dog's actions, not mine, stop the discomfort and reduce the pulling. There is some recent research that shows that dogs who are not well trained and continue the pull on these devices can cause front end damage to the shoulders and legs. So you cannot just rely on the tool; you must teach a replacement behavior using treats to make the new behavior more rewarding than the pulling.

Final thoughts on devices

No matter which one you chose, these tools are no more than crutches to learning. If you do not eventually phase them out, no real learning has taken place. Instead the dog simply knows this thing sucks and if they are wearing it, they had better not pull. So, if you choose to use one, please also choose to teach walking well without wearing one! They are simply a means to an end, and not the result. So on to the first step!

*Think of sled dogs... They pull with their shoulders!

Hand Feeding (Gotta have attention to fix a problem)

I always get one question from folks when they find out I'm a dog trainer. "What can I do to make my dog pay attention to me?" That's a bit like asking what a person can do to get better gas mileage; there are more than just one or two answers!

There is one thing I wish all dog owners would do: Hand feed your dog.

When you hand feed, you become more important to your dog, you teach bite inhibition, and you get your pooch to pay better attention. All without having to be a butthead!! By hand feeding I focus on teaching and rewarding the dog vs. focusing on the mistakes they make and punishing. In a sense I use hand feeding so I don't have to use the outdated ideas of alpha dominance that is still out there in the world of dog training (this will be a recurring theme throughout the book).

Let's break down hand feeding into three smaller ideas to make it easier to understand:

- "I need my human to get food."

Hand feeding makes you more important in your dog's eyes. Some trainers call this "being the pack leader", and others call it "being the alpha dog." I simply call it making yourself the most important and necessary thing in your dog's life. The way I look at leadership with my dogs is if I control all the most important resources in their lives, who is really going to be calling the shots? If I could get people to hand feed every piece of food individually to their dog for at least 30 days, the dog is going to quickly understand that Mom and/or Dad is the key to meal time, and that they had better pay attention when that time comes! This is not only a great way to bond with your dog, this will be your first step in fixing that sore shoulder your pooch is responsible for!

- **Bite inhibition is critical to paying attention.**

I believe that all dogs need to be taught to be gentle with their mouths and teeth when interacting with people. There is no better way to get this point across than by hand feeding. It gives me the perfect opportunity to focus on giving pieces of kibble, one or two at a time, and teaching the command "Gentle". If the dog touches my finger with teeth, I can just say "Ouch," with a calm voice. Then I use the command "Gentle", withhold the food for a moment, then repeat the process. Before you know it, the Land Shark you've been living with will become the polite and patient dog you wanted in the first place! Simply by feeding our dogs by hand, we are teaching mouth skills (or bite inhibition) with humans, who they need for the stuff they want. And this, my friends, will lead to a pooch much more likely to listen when you are talking (or walking, for that matter).

- **Impulse control**

Next we teach the command "Wait". It is similar to "Gentle", only now there is a 3-5 second pause required before Fido can have the piece of kibble. The goal is simple: Patience! Fido needs to learn to pay attention to Mom and Dad, to be gentle and patient.

Most dogs with problem behaviors subscribe to, "I see, I want, I grab... I run!" If we teach Fido to wait a couple of seconds before giving him his kibble, he learns that he still gets what he wants if he can wait just a little bit. It even helps with problem solving: I want dogs to be able to think through challenges, and figure out how to make the rewards more frequent! In other words I want my dog to figure out how to give me what I want, which then leads to what *they* want! Instead of yelling, pleading and punishing the dog, we have to teach them what we want, and let them figure out how to make the right choice.

Final Thoughts on Hand Feeding

Hopefully you are seeing that hand feeding your dog will not only get them to pay attention, but will also jump start *any* training program. Not sure you buy into this idea? Well regardless of whether you are a dog or a person, we all tend to pay way more attention to the people in our lives that give out the rewards, paychecks or praise. Unfortunately the opposite can be said for those who punish, yell or take things away: We usually avoid them like the plague!

So simply by looking at the relationship between you and your dog, and determining who controls the resources, you put yourself right at the top of Fido's list! And if you do it right, training will actually become something fun for both of you! Let's face it, if it ain't fun, you ain't gonna practice (which we both know has to happen).

There is a critical mistake that many people make when trying to control resources with a dog: They think that control must, in some way, be negative. Spoiling a dog or child is thought to be a bad thing, but what if the spoiling only occurs when the dog or child has earned it? The goal is to *be necessary* in their life, not to control that life. So get out there and hand feed your pooch and see the difference it will make!

Do just the hand feeding along with "Gentle" and "Wait" for one to two weeks. Then we can introduce the command "Watch Me".

Watch Me

"Watch Me" should be the first command that people teach their dogs. After hand feeding, what better way is there to teach paying attention than the dog learning to look me in the face? This is exactly what Watch Me is: With either a hand signal or a verbal cue, Fido will stop what he is doing and look to me and wait for the next command. Watch Me can be used for a variety of reasons, but it's the first step in stopping problem behaviors. Dogs can rarely walk and chew bubble gum at the same time, so if Fido is engaging in a behavior I don't like, the first thing I will do is ask for a "Watch Me". For that split second when the dog stops the inappropriate behavior, I have won the battle! The war is teaching the dog an alternative behavior to replace the bad behavior. For example, if my dog is chewing on my favorite pair of shoes, I will first ask for a "Watch Me" (to gain attention) and then ask for a "Sit" (alternative behavior) to take the place of the chewing of my shoes (so I can then put them in the closet where they should have been in the first place).

Get a high value treat* and place it right on the end of your dog's nose, but don't let him have it yet. Once you have the dog's interest, move your hand (with the treat) toward your face and point to your nose with one of your fingers. When your dog gives you eye contact, reward. As the dog becomes more comfortable looking up at your face, begin to shape your verbal signal and say, "Watch Me". I use my middle finger pointing at my nose for my hand signal (because I hold my treat with index and thumb) and simply say the words "Watch Me" as my verbal cue. This command can be used for barking, jumping up, rushing the door and even pulling on the leash! Remember: This command is all about redirecting the dog's attention to you vs. engaging in stuff we don't want!

As you get better with "Watch Me", we need to start asking for a sit as well. Our end result will be that the command "Watch Me" actually *includes* a sit! Once you have "Watch Me" down, don't just offer the treat immediately. Fido will be a little taken aback at first, since eye contact has always gotten him the treat right away. In many cases, they will add the sit automatically at this point, especially if you have been working your sits during training. If not, just quietly ask for a "Sit", then again a "Watch Me". Before you know it, you will be getting your dog to look you in the eye from a sitting position each time you use the command "Watch Me".

Many times, I hear "My dog does not want to look me in the face." Watch Me can be a strange idea to a dog: What does it mean when two dogs lock eyes and don't blink? It's a challenge, and some anxious, shy, fearful or even aggressive dogs may not want to participate in this command. Let me be clear: If you're dealing with aggression, I don't recommend you trying this by yourself. Call a trainer or behaviorist. Remember to relax and go slow. If the dog will only glance at you with the treat, start there, and work towards a more reliable Watch Me. It may take some time, but it will be worth it.

Two skills down, one to go! Then we can actually talk about the leash. Now it's time to teach attention when your back is turned.

*This is a treat that is more exciting than plain old kibble- the higher the treat value, the more attention you have from your best friend! Small, stinky and soft is the key to High Value Treats... Think pieces of hot dog or cheese!

Turn-Around Game

Start by asking for a Watch Me, wait for the sit and give the reward. Then turn your back on the dog, and just wait. As the time builds, the dog should come around to face you. Again: Wait for the sit, reward, and turn your back on the dog. Repeat. At first, you might have to do some luring with the treat to get him to come around to face you, but just go slow and have some fun with the process.

If this is hard for you to visualize in your head, no worries, just look up Kiss Dog Training's YouTube Channel and find the playlist *How-To Stuff With Your Dog* and find the video "Hand Feeding - The Turn-Around Game"... You will get to watch me demonstrate this with my pup, Lexi!

As your dog starts to grasp the Turn-Around Game, it's time to add steps. Do the "Watch Me", get a sit, reward the dog. Then turn around and take two steps away from the dog, and wait for them to come sit in front of you and make eye contact. Before you know it, you will be able to walk all over the house, and wherever you stop, the dog will come front, look at you and sit patiently, waiting for his or her treat, and for you to let them know what comes next!

Trainer's Tip and Warning: It bears repeating: The command "Watch Me" is a fantastic command for basic obedience. However, if you are working with any dog showing fear, anxiety or aggression I strongly recommend professional help with an accredited trainer. Looking a fearful, anxious or aggressive dog in the face/eyes can be construed as a threat or challenge. Do not attempt any of these techniques with aggressive, fearful or anxious dogs without professional help and supervision!

Leash Work in the House

Ok, you know how your dog goes Ape Sh*t every time you pick up the leash, or say the word "walk"? Before we take our new skills on the road, we had better address this behavior, and practice some of our new skills in a manner that will translate to walking a dog. So get out the leash and get ready for the next seven days of practice-walking right in your own home! Because why would your dog pay attention outside, with all the smells and distractions, before they have had the opportunity to practice inside? It may sound boring, but it's a necessary step. Trust me!

Step 1
While the dog is calm, get the leash out. Just start carrying the leash all over the house, and do not put it on the dog until he or she is calm and sitting, and requesting to be hooked up.

Step 2
Hook up the dog and walk five steps at a time, all over your house: Every room, every floor, on the stairs and even in the garage. What's the trick? *Every five steps, you must stop and get an Auto Sit.*

An Auto Sit is a sit that occurs every time you stop on leash. At each stop, the dog flips around front to face you, sits and waits for the next command.

Why have the dog sit facing you versus sitting by your side like so many dog trainers teach*? Because a dog at your side is looking at the whole wide world ahead, which competes with you for his or her attention. Meanwhile a dog that's facing forward and doing a "Watch Me" while sitting is giving you their undivided attention. And a dog who is paying attention is... Not *pulling on the leash*!

So you are to take these five steps and practice the Auto Sits for the next seven days. When you have mastered this step, take your new skills to the next level!

* Also known as a "Heel".

Backyard Building Blocks

Now that you have Auto Sits down, and the work in the house is getting downright boring, we switch things up and head to the pet supply store! I want you to buy a long line: This is a 12-18 feet long leash (remember: I hate retractable leashes, so don't buy one). Then head home to the backyard! Put Fido on the long line and let him or her do whatever he or she wants.

A couple of things could happen:

- The dog doesn't even move- just comes around front and sits, just like you have been practicing! In that case, have a party and reward the crap out of your pooch, and then just walk away.
- The dog tears off like a bullet to begin sniffing everything under the sun in your backyard. In this case simply call the dog back to you and get a front-facing sit, and again reward the crap out of the pooch, and just walk away!
- A combination of these two options, where the dog is interested in checking out the backyard, but staying relatively close. Again, just be patient and wait for the dog to get to the end of the long line and simply call

the dog back, get a front-facing sit, and reward. Repeat after releasing, or walk away from the dog.

What you are doing here is simple: You are building a routine that the length of the long line is your dog's new standard, and as long as the line is loose, Fido is allowed to sniff to his heart's desire. I actually call this ritual checking the Pee-Mail. ☺ In fact I even refer to the actual peeing during this technique as the "Reply All" option. The only real hard and fast rule is that when the dog *reaches the end* of the long line, they must come back, give a front-facing sit, get a treat, and then be released to go back being a dog! Sometimes a bit of freedom goes a long way to fixing problem behaviors.

At the beginning the dog might not really want to explore much, and you will have to either walk away from the dog, or simply quit moving: Either will allow the dog to move away from you, which is our goal so we can then call them back and reward them! It really comes down to your dog feeling comfortable with exploring. As they start being more confident, the opportunities for calling your dog back will increase, just be patient!

The long line is important for two reasons:

1. You've got to let a dog be a dog, and let them sniff! Not all walking can be on a short leash with a ton of rules, or there will be no fun in a walk, and neither of you will enjoy it.
2. Recall* usually ends the fun for the dog! For example:

> "Quit playing with your friends- Come here, we gotta go!" (Not fun)
> "Quit sniffing that and come inside!" (Again, not fun)
> "Don't sniff that butt, quit that and come here!" (Definitely not fun for Fido)

We want to teach the dog that recall is simply checking in, sitting while paying attention, earning a treat, then being released to go back to sniffing and exploring! Over time the dog will realize that recalls are about periodically checking in, versus being micromanaged by the owner. Meanwhile we are still improving leash skills without even realizing it (YET)!

So for the next week or two (until you are rock solid in the backyard), this is where I want you practicing. You are still expected to continue the work inside the house on-leash with the Turn-Around Game, but in the next chapter we talk about the distraction and difficulties of the driveway and the front yard.

*This is what we are really working on with the long line, but it also helps in teaching loose-leash walking.

Driveway Distractions and Front Yard Fiascos

You now have the house down pat with the Turn-Around Game on leash, and you can easily navigate the backyard with a long line, and get a Watch Me with a sit each time the dog gets to the end! Now what? The forbidden fruit of the front yard: The one spot Fido is never allowed off-leash due to the fear or reality of him/her running for the hills! That's because you never truly got that environment "normalized" (or, "no longer exciting"); Fido is usually at his *worst* here! Let's temporarily switch back to the regular leash and take it step by step, making it as easy as we can.

- Start with the Turn-Around Game, but only on the driveway. Every three steps, stop and wait for the front-facing sit. Be patient; the distraction level of the driveway, compared with the house or backyard, is *huge*! You may have to lure the dog into the front-facing sit. You might even want to shift your hand feeding from inside the house to outside at this point. This will give the dog a reason to pay attention to *you* outside on a walk, versus paying attention to the environment. Just be patient, kind and relaxed with the training; just like the house and the backyard, the driveway will also become a normal walking environment. When three

steps are easy and every stop gets an automatic front-facing sit, move to five steps and master that.
- Add the sidewalks in front of your house: Now you are adding a right or left turn at the end of the driveway, and heading toward the neighbors on each side of your house (but no further).
- Next is moving to your front yard on leash: Five steps and stop, then getting the automatic front-facing sit.

By now we should have a rock solid Turn-Around Game in the:

- House
- Backyard (with the long line)
- Driveway
- Sidewalk in front of your house
- Front Yard

Do this 3-5 times a week for two weeks, for about 30 minutes at a time... All the while hand-feeding daily. If you are not willing to put in that much work, don't expect these results. Sorry... No one ever said this would be fast!

Change up the leash to a long line

Do it all again, but this time on the long line! Yep... Start with the driveway and practice the long line recall. Same as the backyard, but now out front! Move to the sidewalks and finally your front yard.

The distraction of the front yard is way higher than anywhere else you have worked. You are going to be near dogs, people, squirrels, cars and all sorts of other distractions. So it is your job to be ready at all times. I usually use my foot as a braking system if the dog heads toward the street: I simply step on the long line, which stops the dog. I also use my foot when we encounter dogs or other people in the beginning so that I can keep the dog near me. This is critical and might even be worth hiring a trainer to work with you until it feels natural (safety first).

Trying to do this without all the prerequisite work in the house, backyard, driveway, sidewalk and front yard (on both long and short leashes) will quite possibly end up with injury to you and/or the dog! If you feel you are not ready for this by yourself, hire a trainer to help show you the tips and tricks: It's money well spent! All that being said, if you have seen or are starting to see aggressive behavior from your dog toward people or other dogs... Long line training is NOT recommended! Call a trainer and get help.

If all goes smoothly in the next week or so of practice, we are finally ready to start (slowly) walking in the neighborhood!

Trainer's Tip for Long Lines:
I use the word "Easy" right before my dog gets to the end of the long line. Then I call my dog to me for the front-facing sit, and a reward. Over time your dog learns not only to slow down on hearing the word "Easy" but will start heading back to you before reaching the end of the long line. This takes practice in ever more distracting environments, but with your commitment and practice you will be amazed at how easy long line training can be. In fact, I would recommend our book How To Get Your Dog To Come Without Being A Butt-head for recall tips.

The actual walking work week

Every four days, add another set of driveways. What do I mean? Well at this point you should be able to walk out of the house, walk around your yard and driveway, and make it to the driveway of each neighbor closest to your house. After four days of practicing that, we are going to add a further driveway in each direction. Practice for another four days, then add yet another driveway to each side, slowly building your walk a little bit at a time.

Not only are you adding more and more distance from home, but also the number of steps between each stop. I would suggest a final goal of stopping every 3-5 minutes so that you never get out of practice with that wonderful front-facing sit. I want you to commit to practicing this routine at least three days a week.

On another two days of the week, I want you to be doing "Pee-Mail" checking on the long line: Same routine, just use the long line instead of the regular leash. If the dog gets to the end of the long line or heads toward the street, stop and call the dog back to you for a front-facing sit, then reward and release. These long line walks will become your dog's opportunity to be a dog, and enjoy the walks a bit!

Remember to use your foot as a brake, and always be aware of your surroundings.

Plan on walking five days a week for about 4-6 weeks, practicing regular leash walking 3 days and doing the "Pee-Mail" walk 2 days a week to reinforce the training. Just remember these two rules:

- On the short (regular) leash, every pull is met with stopping and waiting for a front-facing sit, then a reward before continuing the walk.
- On the long line, every time the dog reaches the end of the line you call the dog back, get a front-facing sit and release them back to being a dog again.

In either case the dog now knows that a *loose* leash is key, and keeps the game going! And that a tight leash means, "Come back, reset or check in." Like I said, dogs only do what works, and we have now taught the dog what makes a walk work for them. Now it's up to us to practice and reward the routine we want! The next chapter talks about how to put it all together in a combo style walk: Both long and short together!

The Combo Walk: Putting it all together!

Now it's time to combine everything you know, and make it all work together! This starts with turning your long line into a combination leash: Tie off loops at every 5 to 6 feet of the long line so that there are 2 to 3 handles on the line. For example, my 25-foot-long line is only about 18 feet, because I tied off two extra handles: I have a handle at about 5 feet, another handle at about 11 feet, and finally the original handle for the full long line that is now about 18 feet.

Why do that? Well, my walks now combine both recall and loose leash walking. I might start off with 20 minutes of long line training, letting my dog sniff and burn off some energy, then I might shorten up to the 5-foot leash and work on some loose leash walking for training purposes, or because maybe I saw a group of joggers headed my way.

By combining the short and long techniques, my dogs are always taking their cue from me as to what kind of work we are doing, which means that they are paying attention to me for cues of what is wanted and what is not. Plus, depending on the situation, I can practice the long line fun walk when the area is quiet, and quickly move to the short leash version if a distraction pops up.

Even with the combo style walk, I only expect you to walk your dog about five days a week. You still have two days a week where you don't have to practice recall or loose leash walking, but don't think you're getting off that easy, because you still have homework on those days, and they include field trips!

Weekend Work

Weekends are your chance and responsibility to tackle distractions! If you buy into my method of teaching a dog how to walk on leash, you should plan to invest about two months of work to see results; but real results come when your dog can handle just about any environment you throw at them, and that comes from going the extra mile... Field trips! Visit the pet store, the hardware store or any other dog-friendly business. Hit up a coffee shop patio or an ice cream shop with your dog.

There are parks where kids practice sports, or places where dog-friendly festivals may be taking place. Heck even in my hometown, the Kansas City Royals do two games a season where you can take your dog! Use weekends to take crazy and distracting field trips, and you will have what we dog trainers call a "Calm-during-the-crazy" dog: These dogs are used to the chaos, they still pay attention in public, and they can handle pretty much all distractions! Perfection isn't the goal: Perfect dogs, kids, bosses or spouses don't really exist, but there are great examples of each that are close to perfect. We put in the time and effort to get to that point in our relationships. That is what I hope this book has shown you: That given time, practice and a little patience, we can teach our dogs what it is we want, versus yelling and screaming about what we don't!

Good luck, and remember to Keep it Simple Stupid, and don't forget to have a little fun while you're at it!

Mike

My Warranty Statement

Okay so we've covered everything about why and how to fix your dog's leash pulling habit, but I must reiterate two words: **Frequency** and **Consistency**. If you are not frequently consistent or consistently frequent with the things I teach you, you're going to be disappointed in the results that you get from working with me. This has been my warranty statement since the day I started my business. It's why I don't like being called The Dog Trainer, and would rather be known as The People-Who-Own-Dogs Trainer. It's not the dogs I have to train: It's *you*! People rarely tend to be consistent or frequent with anything – I'm guilty of it too! Let's face it, this is the reason why diets, working out, quitting smoking or any other resolution seem to be so damn hard!

I always include this chapter as a reminder to have fair expectations of what your dog will and will not do. Animals are not computers, machines or things that can be controlled. Dogs are simply beings whom we want to share our lives with! Don't look to control the dog that you live with; instead, learn to *teach* the dog that you live with. In the end, I think both of you will be happier for it.

One final note on the training you'll be doing: The word *Fun* is very important in everyone's life, your dog's included. If the training you do is militant, controlling or difficult, neither you nor the dog will enjoy it. And ironically, neither of you will learn from it. Think back to your own educational background. Did you learn more from the classes that you enjoyed or from the ones that you hated? Don't forget to have fun! That's probably what you were looking for when you decided to bring a dog into your house. I wish you all the luck in the world, but know that it has way more to do with consistency and frequency than luck!

Conclusion

Well you made it, folks: The end of the book! First, I want to say thanks for buying it. Secondly, I really hope that you learned something here in these pages that will help you and your dog to communicate better. The information in these pages has come from many years of helping folks with dogs who like to pull on the leash just a little too much. I promise that if you put in the time and practice *with* your dog (versus against your dog), really anything can be accomplished. If you enjoyed the book, there's plenty more available: We have several other books, videos (YouTube channel: Mike Deathe), an active blog, a Facebook page and other social media outlets. We love to teach folks to speak Dog as a Second Language!

While writing these books has been a pleasure, my true passion is public speaking. I love spreading the word about positive, scientific-based dog training. There are many people out there who have no idea how simple it is to train a dog, or how enjoyable it can be! So simply Google me, Mike Deathe, or visit our business page, www.kissdogtraining.com [http://www.kissdogtraining.com], if you or your group would like to have me come give a presentation.

A final request, if you don't mind: As a small author, one of the greatest gifts that you the reader can give me is a few minutes of your time to do an online review of this book. I just need your support to get the word out! Thank you for buying the book, thank you for reading the book, and thank you for being a part of training your dog the *Keep It Simple Stupid* way!

Mike

www.ingramcontent.com/pod-product-compliance
Lightning Source LLC
Chambersburg PA
CBHW052043070526
44584CB00018B/2594